DOCTRINAL STATEMENTS OF THE WELS

Prepared by the Commission on Inter-Church Relations
of the Wisconsin Evangelical Lutheran Synod, 1997

EDITORIAL NOTES

The doctrinal statements in this booklet are not being reproduced primarily as historical documents. They are being reprinted, rather, in the hope that they will serve as guides for study of Scripture and will help us make the truths they contain our own personal convictions. We have used the New International Version for all biblical quotes, therefore, to make them clearer and easier to understand for the modern-day reader.

Since these doctrinal statements were written over a span of more than 30 years, it is not surprising that in their original form they contain stylistic differences in punctuation and capitalization. In the interest of consistency and readability we have changed capitalization and punctuation as needed.

In the doctrinal statements we have capitalized pronouns which refer to God because the majority of the originals did so. In the introductory sections we have followed current usage and not capitalized the pronouns.

All quotes from the Lutheran Confessions throughout this booklet are from the *Concordia Triglotta*.

TABLE OF CONTENTS

Introduction   1

Statement on Scripture   5

Statement on the Antichrist   13

Theses on Church Fellowship   25

Theses on the Church and Ministry   39

Resolution on Abortion   53

Statement on the Lord's Supper   57

Scriptural Principles of Man and Woman Roles   61

INTRODUCTION

In this booklet we are confessing articles of faith, truths revealed by God in the Holy Scriptures. Even a brief look at the size and contents of the booklet, however, will show this is not a listing of everything we believe and teach on the basis of the Bible. A word of explanation, therefore, is appropriate to indicate why these relatively few statements are here printed.

As a synod we do not formulate doctrinal declarations on a regular basis. We confess the full inspiration and inerrancy of the Scriptures and their binding authority in all matters of doctrine. The three ecumenical creeds, the primary creedal statements of historic Christianity, summarize well our faith. In addition, we wholeheartedly subscribe to the Lutheran Confessions (contained in the *Book of Concord* of 1580) because they are correct expositions of biblical truth. Since our Christian and Evangelical Lutheran forefathers have bequeathed us such accurate and comprehensive doctrinal affirmations, we seldom feel the need to draft additional ones.

The seven documents in this booklet are doctrinal declarations that have been formally endorsed by our synod in the 20th century. For those unfamiliar with who we are and what we stand for, our church body has also prepared a pamphlet with the title *This We Believe* to summarize what we believe and teach. This pamphlet is intended primarily as a tool for teaching and for evangelism.

To demonstrate the point that we have drafted few doctrinal statements, consider theological truths that are not addressed in this publication. What we hold to be the primary or central Bible teachings are not directly addressed in the statements presented here. For example, no affirmations of the Triune God, the deity of Jesus Christ, the vicarious atonement of Christ, or his second coming are included. We are quick to assure our readers that we wholeheartedly embrace and cherish these and other historic Christian doctrines. We especially affirm and confess the truth of justification by grace alone and through faith alone as the chief doctrine of Scripture and the heart of God's gospel of salvation for sinful mankind. If our gracious God had not brought us to know and trust the fact that he has reconciled us to himself in Christ, all other doctrines and doctrinal statements would ultimately mean nothing to us.

Why then has the Wisconsin Synod formulated these particular doctrinal statements? A reader will notice that many of the statements deal with subjects not fully or explicitly addressed in the Lutheran Confessions. So to a degree we felt the need to supplement what the forefathers wrote. G. K. Chesterton is quoted as saying that "truths turn into dogma the moment they are disputed." We acknowledge that the dogma here published was occasioned by controversy either in our own synodical dealings or in the society in which we live. We shall always find necessity and value in confessing the truth in the face of error. Part of our Christian responsibility is to clarify the truth when confronted by questions, and to affirm the truth as an encouragement to those who struggle against falsehood. These doctrinal statements testify that our synod saw the need to set forth the truth in the face of controversy at various times in its history. It is not at all surprising that Christians must testify in this way during their earthly pilgrimage. What is perhaps surprising is that our synod has formulated relatively few declarations and that these are relatively brief. We hold this to be a testimony to God's grace in keeping us largely united in the confession of his truths and largely free from doctrinal controversies and struggles, especially on the primary doctrines of the Bible. We invite our readers to share our joy in this.

We also want to make clear our purpose in having these statements printed at this time. We see value for those in our own midst that the review of often-debated doctrines may stimulate renewed study of the Bible. This in turn, under the Holy Spirit's blessing, will result in convictions and harmony that keep us united in God's truth. A closely related benefit is to testify to the world what we believe and why. If what we publicly declare will in any way bring people to examine and ponder what God has graciously said in Scripture, we rejoice. We desire to share freely what we have so freely received. May we always be enabled to speak the truth and to speak it in love that the spiritual upbuilding of God's people might result among us and others.

In the brief introductions to the various confessional statements, a reader may come across references to essays and doctrinal treatises. The actual synodical resolutions, as well as the reports which fill in the historical background, are found in the *Proceedings* and *Book of Reports and Memorials* of the pertinent conventions. Access to these may be gained through the libraries at our ministerial education college and theological seminary, Martin Luther College in New Ulm, Minnesota, and Wisconsin Lutheran Seminary in Mequon, Wisconsin.

People must be brought to love and trust the truth in addition to knowing it. We look to the Holy Spirit to accomplish this gracious work in our hearts and yours.

Commission on Inter-Church Relations
Wisconsin Evangelical Lutheran Synod

STATEMENT ON SCRIPTURE

Introduction to the Statement

Differences in doctrine and practice among the members of the Synodical Conference were beginning to surface already in the 1930s and 1940s. These differences threatened the fellowship our Wisconsin Synod had enjoyed with the other church bodies of the Synodical Conference since 1872. Meeting in Saginaw, Michigan, the 1955 WELS convention, by unanimous vote, adopted the Preamble to the Report of Floor Committee No. 2. This Preamble identified the specific doctrinal issues in controversy.

Now the following needed to be determined: Was the Missouri Synod a weak brother in need of our admonition? Would the synod respond to our patient, brotherly admonition? If this were the case, we had a responsibility to bring loud and clear admonition to our weak brother. Or was Missouri set in its unscriptural doctrines and practices? Were we compelled reluctantly to regard Missouri as those "who cause divisions and put obstacles in your way that are contrary to the teaching you have learned" (Ro 16:17)? In such a case the God-pleasing course was clear: "keep away from them"; we must terminate fellowship with Missouri.

The 1955 convention was not sure which of the above two possibilities was the case. It voted, therefore, to recess the convention for one year. The recessed session in 1956 still did not feel it was able to make a judgment. It voted to "hold in abeyance the judgment of our Saginaw resolutions until the next convention." The Standing Committee on Matters of Church Union was instructed to "continue to evaluate any further developments in these matters."

The Synodical Conference convention at Chicago, Illinois, on December 4–7, 1956, adopted resolutions calling for the Union Committees of the member synods to meet for future discussions in the hope of reaching agreement in the controversial issues. The 1957 Wisconsin Synod convention concurred that such doctrinal discussions should continue "in an effort to restore full unity on the basis of the Word of God."

The Wisconsin Synod's Standing Committee on Church Union at this time included the synod's president and vice presidents, all district presidents as well as all members of the seminary faculty. A subcommittee of eight was chosen to attend the meetings of the Joint Union Committees on behalf of the Wisconsin Synod. President Oscar Naumann led the delegation. In all, six meetings were held in 1957, 1958, and 1959. Each meeting was scheduled for three days.

The second meeting, in Chicago on April 22–24, 1957, took up the first subject agreed upon for discussion. All four synods (Missouri, Slovak, Wisconsin, and Evangelical Lutheran Synod) made presentations on Scripture—Revelation, Inspiration, Principles of Interpretation, and Open Questions.

These discussions did not take place in a vacuum. In 1957 another committee was busily working in the United States to draft a statement on Scripture. The Joint Commission on Lutheran Unity, representing the United Lutheran Church in America, the Augustana Evangelical Lutheran Church, the Finnish Evangelical Lutheran Church (= Suomi Synod), and the American Evangelical Lutheran Church, was at work. Its statement was to be used as the doctrinal basis for the proposed merger into the Lutheran Church in America. On December 16, 1957, the Joint Commission's draft was released. Words such as inspired and inerrant were missing from that document. Rather, it stated that these church bodies "treasure the Holy Scriptures . . . as the primary witness to God's redemptive act in Christ." It spoke of "the Gospel transmitted by the Holy Scriptures" as the true treasure of the Church and said: "The Holy Spirit uses the Church's witness to the Gospel to create Christian faith and fellowship." In other words, the statement of the future LCA deemed it sufficient to confess that the Scriptures contain the Word of God. It limited the authority of Scripture to the Gospel message rather than say that everything in the Bible is true.

In contrast to this, the result of the second meeting of the Joint Union Committees of the Synodical Conference was positive. After thorough discussion of the subject of Scripture by representatives of the four synods, there was full agreement in substance. The "Statement on Scripture" was prepared. It was approved by the convention of the Synodical Conference in 1958. And in turn it was adopted by the Wisconsin Synod, without a dissenting voice, in its 1959 convention. The other three church bodies of the Synodical Conference also adopted it in their conventions.

The discussions within the Synodical Conference had begun on a hopeful note. Now there was a basis to address other issues in controversy because all agreed that the Scripture would serve as the inerrant guide and absolute authority for the discussions.

No true unity and no doctrinal clarity can come without acceptance of the Scripture as the inspired and inerrant Word of God. Thus the "Statement on Scripture" remains an important and timeless document for our church.

Statement on Scripture

I. Introduction

God reveals Himself to men primarily through His incarnate Son, whom He attests and presents to His Church through

Scripture. The purpose of Scripture is to proclaim Christ as the Savior of sinners (Jn 5:39,46; Ac 10:43). All Scripture is written because of Christ and has a connection with the revelation of God in Christ, some passages directly, some more remotely. Every word of Scripture is therefore an organic part of the Scripture's witness to Christ. And Scripture is the complete message of God to sinners. By it man is freed from carnal security and self-righteousness, is delivered from despair, and regains by faith the lost image of God. Gal 3:26; cf. 4:31; Jas 1:18; 1 Pe 1:23; Jn 8:31,32.

We reject the idea that the natural knowledge of God is sufficient to salvation or useful beyond the use made of it in Scripture (Ro 1:20; 2:1,14-16; Ac 17:22,23). The revelation of God in nature and conscience is insufficient for salvation because man by reason of his fall is so constituted that he persistently perverts and distorts the revelation given to him by God and refuses to acknowledge or to submit to the God who thus reveals Himself. And man pursuing this perverted course is either led to feel secure in his self-righteousness or is driven to despair.

We reject the idea that tradition is a source of revelation. Cf. Mt 15:3-6; Col 2:8.

We reject the idea that other new sources or norms of divine revelation besides Scripture are to be expected. Heb 1:1,2; Mt 28:19,20; Gal 1:8,9.

II. The Inspiration of Scripture

We believe and teach that all Scripture (that is, all the canonical books of the Old and New Testaments) is given by inspiration of God and is in its entirety, in its parts, and in its very words inspired by the Holy Spirit. God revealed Himself personally and directly to such men as Adam, Abraham, Moses, and the prophets. Some of these He called to transmit His message to men orally or in writing. Their message was thus not their own, but God's Word. They were moved by the Holy Spirit, so that He is the true Author of their every word. Inspiration means, then, that mighty act of God whereby He spoke His Word in the words of men and made them the effective and final vehicle of His revelation. Hence these words do not merely inform us concerning God's past action; they also convey God's action now. 1 Th 2:13; 2 Pe 1:19-21; 2 Ti 3:15-17; 1 Co 2:13; Jer 23:29; Ro 1:16,17.

In giving men His message by inspiration, God had men express His Word in their own language (Hebrew, Aramaic, or Greek), and in their own style (personal, historical, poetic, oratorical). (Cf. the superscription on the cross, Mt 27:37; Mk 15:26; Lk 23:38; Jn 19:19,20.) Thus the holy writers felt personally responsible for every word they wrote (cf. 2 Co 7:8), while they at the same time knew that their words were given by the Holy Spirit (1 Co 2:12,13).

We reject as a distortion of the true conception of verbal inspiration any idea which makes the act of inspiration a mere mechanical dictation.

We condemn and reject any and all teachings and statements that would limit the inerrancy and sufficiency of Scripture, or that deny the divine authorship of certain portions of Scripture. Inspiration applies not only to such statements as speak directly of Christ, but also to such as may seem very remote (e.g., in the field of history, geography, and nature). For since God is the Lord of history and has revealed Himself by acts in history and has in the person of His Son actually entered into man's history, the historical framework in which the Gospel message is set in Scripture is an essential part of the inspired Word just as much as the spiritual truths revealed in it.

We reject the idea that verbal inspiration is called into question by accidents in the transmission of the text and the resultant variants in the manuscripts. Inspiration pertains in the first instance to the original autographs of Scripture. But by His gracious providence God has given us such a fullness and variety of witnesses to the original text that Christian scholarship reproduces it with great fidelity. God has so watched over the transmission of the text that the variant readings nowhere affect the doctrines of Scripture. We gratefully acknowledge also that translations of Scripture, though not under particular inspiration, are by God's providential care adequate vehicles of His revelation in the inspired Word. Heb 2:3; 1 Pe 1:25; Mk 13:31; Jn 17:20; Mt 28:19,20.

III. The Authority of Scripture

We believe and teach that God has given us His Holy Scripture to make us wise unto salvation through faith in Christ Jesus (2 Ti 3:13-17). We therefore confess Scripture to be the only, but all-sufficient foundation of our faith, the source of all our teachings, the norm of our conduct in life, and the infallible authority in all matters with which it deals. Lk 16:29-31; Dt 4:2; 13:1-5; Isa 8:20; Ac 26:22; Jn 10:35.

We believe and teach that where Scripture has not spoken decisively or is silent, differences of opinion may be held without violating Scripture or breaking the bonds of fellowship. Such matters fall into the area called "open questions." Scripture itself must determine which questions are to be considered as open. The term "open questions" may legitimately be used where the Scripture language leaves open the precise scope of a passage, or where linguistic, textual or historical problems make the perception of the intended sense difficult. But where Scripture has spoken, there God has spoken, whether it be on a central dogma or on a peripheral point; where Scripture has not spoken, the matter must forever remain open. 1 Pe 4:11; Jer 23:22,23.

Scripture being the Word of God, it carries its own authority in itself and does not receive it by the approbation of the

Church. The Canon, that is, that collection of books which is the authority for the Church, is not the creation of the Church. Rather, the Canon has, by a quiet historical process which took place in the worship life of the Church, imposed itself upon the Church by virtue of its own divine authority.

IV. The Interpretation of Scripture

Since Scripture is God's Word, the interpretation of Scripture should not be regarded as merely or primarily an intellectual task. The true meaning of Scripture becomes clear for man in a given situation, not merely by a scrupulous study of Scripture and a careful analysis of the facts at issue, but rather by approaching Scripture in a spirit of repentance and faith which makes men obedient sons of God, who hear Scripture when it speaks as Law in all the rigidity of the Law, and when it speaks as Gospel in all the unconditional grace of the Gospel. 2 Co 4:3,4; 2 Ti 3:16,17; Gal 2:5; 5:3,6.

Scripture alone is to interpret Scripture. The hermeneutical rule that Scripture must be interpreted according to the rule, or the analogy, of faith means that the clear passages of Scripture, not any theological system or dogmatical summary of Bible doctrine, are to determine the interpretation. Seemingly obscure passages must not be interpreted so as to pervert or contradict clear passages. This means that every statement of Scripture must be understood in its native sense, according to grammar, context, and linguistic usage of the time. Where Scripture speaks historically, as for example in Genesis 1–3, it must be understood as speaking of literal, historical facts. Where Scripture speaks symbolically, metaphorically or metonymically, as for example in Revelation 20, it must be interpreted on these its own terms. Furthermore, since God spoke in the common language of men, expressions such as sunrise and sunset, the corners of the earth, etc., must not be viewed as intending to convey scientific information. Ps 119:105; 2 Pe 1:19; 2 Ti 3:15.

Since the same God speaks by the same creative energy of the same Holy Spirit throughout Scripture, the Old Testament and the New Testament are to be viewed as constituting an organic unity. This unity is to be understood, not as a simple equation of the two testaments with each other, but in the sense of Hebrews 1:1,2: "In the past God spoke to our forefathers through the prophets at many times and in various ways, but in these last days he has spoken to us by his Son." Since the New Testament is the culminating revelation of God, it is decisive in determining the relation between the two testaments and the meaning of the Old Testament prophecies in particular; the meaning of a prophecy becomes known in full only from its fulfillment.

Since Scripture is in all its parts and in all its words the inspired Word of God, we reject and condemn any use of the phrase "totality of Scripture" which tends to abridge or annul the force of any clear passage of Scripture. Similarly we reject the use of any phrase which makes room for the idea that the Scripture as a whole may be regarded as the Word of God, though it in many details is regarded as only the words of men.

We reject and condemn "demythologizing" as a denial of the Word of God. Where Scripture records as historical facts those events and deeds which far surpass the ordinary experience of men, that record must be understood literally, as a record of facts; the miraculous and mysterious may not be dismissed as intended to have only a metaphorical or symbolical meaning.

STATEMENT ON THE ANTICHRIST

Introduction to the Statement

As Martin Luther grew in his appreciation of the gospel, he also grew in his recognition that the Papacy is the Antichrist. A 1954 WELS pamphlet entitled *Antichrist* put it this way: "It was because Luther cherished the Gospel so dearly that his faith instinctively recoiled and protested in unmistakable terms when the Pope put himself in the place of Christ and declared His work insufficient and in vain. That is the use to which Luther's faith put the prophecy of Scripture. For him the tenet that the Pope is the Antichrist was an article of faith."

Luther left no doubt where he stood concerning the Papacy when he wrote, "This teaching [of the supremacy of the pope] shows forcefully that the Pope is the very Antichrist, who has exalted himself above, and opposed himself against Christ, because he will not permit Christians to be saved without his power, which, nevertheless, is nothing, and is neither ordained nor commanded by God. This is, properly speaking, to exalt himself above all that is called God. . . . The Pope, however, prohibits this faith, saying that to be saved a person must obey him" (Smalcald Articles, II, IV, 10-12).

In the centuries after Luther's death, Lutherans accepted this confessional statement without reservation or qualification. In the 1860s, however, doubts about this confessional statement were raised within Lutheranism. They arose from the Iowa Synod, which refused to grant doctrinal status to the teaching that the Papacy is the Antichrist. They listed this teaching under the category of "open questions." The Missouri Synod took the lead, at that time, in defending the view of the Lutheran Confessions that the prophecies of Antichrist have been fulfilled in the Papacy.

The Iowa Synod, however, in a 1904 document continued to teach the view that it is a "human application" of the teaching of Scripture to declare the Papacy to be the Antichrist. The Iowa Synod became part of the American Lutheran Church, and its teaching on the Antichrist persisted in the new union. Since 1930 the ALC taught that it is only a "historical judgment" that the Papacy is the Antichrist. In 1938 this view was officially sanctioned in the ALC "Sandusky Declaration." It stated:

> . . . we accept the historical judgment of Luther in the Smalcald Articles . . . that the Pope is the Antichrist . . . because among all the antichristian manifestations in the history of the world and the Church that lie *behind us in the past* there is none that fits the description given in 2 Thess. 2 better than the Papacy . . .
>
> The answer to the question whether in the *future that is still before us*, prior to the return of Christ, a special unfolding and a personal concentration of the antichristian power already present now, and thus a still more comprehensive fulfillment of 2 Thess. 2 may occur, we leave to the Lord and Ruler of Church and world history (VI, B, 1).

In its "Brief Statement" of 1932 the Missouri Synod repudiated the teaching that the identification of the Papacy as the Antichrist is only a historical judgment. It declared, "The prophecies of the Holy Scriptures concerning the Antichrist . . . have been fulfilled in the Pope of Rome and his dominion." It subscribed "to the statement of our Confessions that the Pope is 'the very Antichrist.'" It declared that the doctrine of Antichrist is "not to be included in the number of open questions" (43, 44).

As time went on, however, the Missouri Synod began to retreat from its previous position. In 1951, the Report of the

Advisory Committee on Doctrine and Practice of the Lutheran Church—Missouri Synod stated:

> Scripture does not teach that the Pope is the Antichrist. It teaches that there will be an Antichrist (prophecy). We identify the Antichrist as the Papacy. This is an historical judgment based on Scripture. The early Christians could not have identified the Antichrist as we do. If there were a clearly expressed teaching of Scripture, they must have been able to do so. Therefore the quotation from *Lehre und Wehre* [in 1904 by Dr. Stoeckhardt which identifies the Papacy as Antichrist] goes too far.

This view was endorsed by the Lutheran Church—Missouri Synod Convention in Houston in 1953.

It was in this setting, then, that the "Statement on the Antichrist" was drafted. The Joint Doctrinal Committees of the Synodical Conference adopted this statement on October 15, 1958, and reported this to the Lutheran Synodical Conference Convention in 1960. The "Statement on the Antichrist" was adopted by the Wisconsin Evangelical Lutheran Synod at its convention in Saginaw, Michigan, in 1959, without a dissenting vote. The Missouri Synod, however, never formally adopted it.

In conclusion, we quote a statement from an essay written in 1957 which puts this doctrine into proper perspective:

> This teaching that the Papacy is the Antichrist is not a fundamental article of faith. . . . It is not an article on which saving faith rests, with which Christianity stands or falls. We cannot and do not deny the Christianity of a person who cannot see the truth that the Pope is the Antichrist.
>
> Yet it is an important article and should not be side-stepped or slighted. It is clearly revealed in the divine word, and there is nothing needless and useless in the Bible; God wants us to know about the Antichrist. . . . This article is clearly expressed in the Lutheran Confessions; whoever denies it does not stand in one faith with his fathers; he is not a confessional Lutheran. A Lutheran preacher should know, believe, and teach this article or frankly confess that he no longer subscribes to the Confessions of

the Lutheran Church. If we value the saving doctrine of the vicarious atonement through the blood of Jesus Christ, the God-man, in these latter days of the world, we shall do well to keep the facts concerning the Antichrist well in mind ("The Scriptural Doctrine of the Antichrist," *Our Great Heritage*, Vol. 3, pp. 601,602).

Statement on the Antichrist

I.

Scripture speaks of many forces and powers which are actively hostile to Christ and His Church, and uses the term "antichrist" with reference to some of them.

Da 11:36-38; Mt 24:22-25; 1 Ti 4:1-3; 2 Ti 3:1-9; 1 Jn 2:18-22 —compare the whole passage, 18-23; 1 Jn 4:1-6; 2 Jn 7; 2 Th 2:1-12, compare also 13-17.

These and similar passages reveal to the Church that antichristian forces will appear in various recurrent forms until the end of time.

II.

Scripture, however, speaks also of a particular personal embodiment of the antichristian power in which the iniquity of false teaching finds its climax (2 Th 2:1-12):

> [1]Concerning the coming of our Lord Jesus Christ and our being gathered to him, we ask you, brothers, [2]not to become easily unsettled or alarmed by some prophecy, report or letter supposed to have come from us, saying that the day of the Lord has already come. [3]Don't let anyone deceive you in any way, for that day will not come until the rebellion occurs and the man of lawlessness is revealed, the man doomed to destruction. [4]He will oppose and will exalt himself over everything that is called God or is worshiped, so that he sets himself up in God's temple, proclaiming himself to be God.
>
> [5]Don't you remember that when I was with you I used to tell you these things? [6]And now you know what is holding him back, so

that he may be revealed at the proper time. [7]For the secret power of lawlessness is already at work; but the one who now holds it back will continue to do so till he is taken out of the way. [8]And then the lawless one will be revealed, who the Lord Jesus will overthrow with the breath of his mouth and destroy by the splendor of his coming. [9]The coming of the lawless one will be in accordance with the work of Satan displayed in all kinds of counterfeit miracles, signs and wonders, [10]and in every sort of evil that deceives those who are perishing. They perish because they refused to love the truth and so be saved. [11]For this reason God sends them a powerful delusion so that they will believe the lie [12]and so that all will be condemned who have not believed the truth but have delighted in wickedness.

It is with this aspect of the antichristian power that the Lutheran Confessions deal under the term "antichrist," and we in a reaffirmation of the Lutheran faith are so using the term.

Passages from the Lutheran Confessions dealing with the subject of the Antichrist:

Apology XV, 18,19:

And what need is there of words on a subject so manifest? If the adversaries defend these human services as meriting justification, grace, and the remission of sins, they simply establish the kingdom of Antichrist. For the kingdom of Antichrist is a new service of God, devised by human authority rejecting Christ, just as the kingdom of Mahomet has services and works through which it wishes to be justified before God; nor does it hold that men are gratuitously justified before God by faith, for Christ's sake. Thus the Papacy also will be a part of the kingdom of Antichrist if it thus defends human services as justifying. For the honor is taken away from Christ when they teach that we are not justified gratuitously by faith, for Christ's sake, but by such services; especially when they teach that such services are not only useful for justification, but are also necessary, as they hold above in Art. VII, where they condemn us for saying that unto true unity of the Church it is not necessary that rites instituted by men should everywhere be alike. Daniel 11:38 indicates that new human services will be the very form and constitution of the kingdom of Antichrist. For he says thus: "But in his estate shall he honor the god of forces; and a god whom his fathers knew not shall he honor with gold and silver and precious stones."

Apology XXIV, 97,98:

Carnal men cannot endure that alone to the sacrifice of Christ the honor is ascribed that it is a propitiation, because they do not understand the righteousness of faith, but ascribe equal honor to the rest of the services and sacrifices. Just as, therefore, in Judah among the godless priests a false opinion concerning sacrifices inhered; just as in Israel, Baalitic services continued, and nevertheless, a Church of God was there which disapproved of godless services, so Baalitic worship inheres in the domain of the Pope, namely, the abuse of the Mass, which they apply, that by it they may merit for the unrighteous the remission of guilt and punishment. [And yet, as God still kept His Church, i.e., some saints, in Israel and Judah, so God still preserved His Church, i.e., some saints, under the Papacy, so that the Christian Church has not entirely perished.] And it seems that this Baalitic worship will endure as long as the reign of the Pope, until Christ will come to judge, and by the glory of His advent destroy the reign of Antichrist.

Smalcald Articles II, II, 25:

The invocation of saints is also one of the abuses of Antichrist conflicting with the chief article, and destroys the knowledge of Christ. Neither is it commanded nor counseled, nor has it any example [or testimony] in Scripture, and even though it were a precious thing, as it is not [while, on the contrary, it is a most harmful thing], in Christ we have everything a thousandfold better [and surer, so that we are not in need of calling upon the saints].

Smalcald Articles II, IV, 10-14, (cf. also Formula of Concord, Solid Declaration, X, 20):

This teaching shows forcefully that the Pope is the very Antichrist, who has exalted himself above, and opposed himself against Christ, because he will not permit Christians to be saved without his power, which, nevertheless, is nothing, and is neither ordained nor commanded by God. This is, properly speaking, to exalt himself above all that is called God, as Paul says (2 Th 2:4). Even the Turks or the Tartars, great enemies of Christians as they are, do not do this, but they allow whoever wishes to believe in Christ, and take bodily tribute and obedience from Christians.

The Pope, however, prohibits this faith, saying that to be saved a person must obey him. This we are unwilling to do, even though on this account we must die in God's name. This all proceeds from the fact that the Pope has wished to be called the supreme head of the Christian Church by divine right. Accordingly he had to make himself equal and superior to Christ, and had to cause himself to be proclaimed the head and then the lord of the Church, and finally of the whole world, and simply God on earth, until he has dared to issue commands even to the angels in heaven. And when we distinguish the Pope's teaching from, or measure and hold it against, Holy Scripture, it is found [it appears plainly] that the Pope's teaching, where it is best, has been taken from the imperial and heathen law, and treats of political matters and decisions or rights as the Decretals show; furthermore, it teaches of ceremonies concerning churches, garments, food, persons and (similar) puerile, theatrical, and comical things without measure, but in all these things nothing at all of Christ, faith, and the commandments of God. Lastly, it is nothing else than the devil himself, because above and against God he urges [and disseminates] his [papal] falsehoods concerning masses, purgatory, the monastic life, one's own works and [fictitious] divine worship (for this is the very Papacy) [upon each of which the Papacy is altogether founded and is standing,] and condemns, murders and tortures all Christians who do not exalt and honor these abominations [of the Pope] above all things. Therefore, just as little as we can worship the devil himself as Lord and God, we can endure his apostle, the Pope, or Antichrist, in his rule as head or lord. For to lie and to kill, and to destroy body and soul eternally, that is wherein his papal government really consists, as I have very clearly shown in many books.

Treatise on the Power and Primacy of the Pope 39-41:

Now, it is manifest that the Roman pontiffs, with their adherents, defend [and practice] godless doctrines and godless services. And the marks [all the vices] of Antichrist plainly agree with the kingdom of the Pope and his adherents. For Paul, 2 Th 2:3, in describing to the Thessalonians Antichrist, calls him "an adversary of Christ, who opposeth and exalteth himself above all that is called God or that is worshiped, so that he as God sitteth in the temple of God." He speaks therefore of one ruling in the Church, not of heathen kings, and he calls this one the adversary of Christ, because he will devise doctrine conflicting with the Gospel and will assume to himself divine authority.

Moreover, it is manifest, in the first place, that the Pope rules in the Church, and by the pretext of ecclesiastical authority and of the ministry has established for himself this kingdom. For he assigns as a pretext these words: "I will give to thee the keys." Secondly, the doctrine of the Pope conflicts in many ways with the Gospel, and [thirdly] the Pope assumes to himself divine authority in a threefold manner. First, because he takes to himself the right to change the doctrine of Christ and services instituted by God, and wants his own doctrine and his own services to be observed as divine; secondly, because he takes to himself the power not only of binding and loosing in this life, but also the jurisdiction over souls after this life; thirdly, because the Pope does not want to be judged by the Church or by anyone, and puts his own authority ahead of the decision of Councils and the entire Church. But to be unwilling to be judged by the Church or by anyone is to make oneself God. Lastly, these errors so horrible, and this impiety, he defends with the greatest cruelty, and puts to death those dissenting.

This being the case, all Christians ought to beware of becoming partakers of the godless doctrine, blasphemies, and unjust cruelty of the Pope. On this account they ought to desert and execrate the Pope with his adherents as the kingdom of Antichrist; just as Christ has commanded, Mt 7:15: "Beware of false prophets." And Paul commands that godless teachers should be avoided and execrated as cursed, Gal 1:8; Tit 3:10; and in 2 Co 6:14 he says: "Be ye not unequally yoked together with unbelievers: For what communion hath light with darkness?"

Treatise on the Power and Primacy of the Pope 57:

Therefore, even though the bishop of Rome had the primacy by divine right, yet since he defends godless services and doctrine conflicting with the Gospel, obedience is not due him; yea, it is necessary to resist him as Antichrist. The errors of the Pope are manifest and not trifling.

III.

The passage (2 Th 2:1-12) promises that God will reveal the "man of lawlessness" and states the tokens, or marks, by means of which God will reveal him to the eyes of faith.

Among these marks are:

1. He "sets himself up in God's temple, proclaiming himself to be God" (2 Th 2:4). He is a religious power demanding religious allegiance, usurping authority in the Church and tyrannizing Christian consciences. Cf. Smalcald Articles II, IV, 10-14.
2. He is an embodiment of Satanic power. This is manifested:
   a. in the fact that he appears as the one who "will oppose and will exalt himself over everything that is called God" (2 Th 2:4). He is God's Adversary;
   b. and in the fact that his opposition to God is an opposition of disguise and deceit. He opposes God by usurping the place and name of God (2 Th 2:4). The Satanic appears, characteristically, in religious form: the "coming" of Antichrist is pitted against the "coming" of Christ, his signs and lying wonders against the miracles of Christ, faith in his lie against faith in the truth of Christ (2 Th 2:10-11).

IV.

Therefore on the basis of a renewed study of the pertinent Scriptures we reaffirm the statement of the Lutheran Confessions, that "the Pope is the very Antichrist" (cf. Section II), especially since he anathematizes the doctrine of the justification by faith alone and sets himself up as the infallible head of the Church.

We thereby affirm that we identify this "Antichrist" with the Papacy as it is known to us today, which shall, as 2 Thessalonians 2:8 states, continue to the end of time, whatever form or guise it may take. This neither means nor implies a blanket condemnation of all members of the Roman Catholic Church, for despite all the errors taught in that church the Word of God is still heard there, and that Word is an effectual Word. Isa 55:10, 11; cf. Apology XXIV, 98, cited above under II.

We make this confession in the confidence of faith. The Antichrist cannot deceive us if we remain under the revelation given us in the Apostolic word (2 Th 2:13-17), for in God's gracious governance of history the Antichrist can deceive only those who "refused to love the truth" (2 Th 2:10-12).

And we make this confession in the confidence of hope. The Antichrist shall not destroy us but shall himself be destroyed—"Whom the Lord Jesus will overthrow with the breath of his mouth and destroy by the splendor of his coming" (2 Th 2:8).

We reject the idea that the fulfillment of this prophecy is to be sought in the workings of any merely secular political power (2 Th 2:4; cf. Treatise on the Power and the Primacy of the Pope 39).

We reject the idea that the teaching that the Papacy is the Antichrist rests on a merely human interpretation of history or is an open question. We hold rather that this teaching rests on the revelation of God in Scripture which finds its fulfillment in history. The Holy Spirit reveals this fulfillment to the eyes of faith (cf. *The Abiding Word*, Vol. 2, p. 764). Since Scripture teaches that the Antichrist would be revealed and gives the marks by which the Antichrist is to be recognized (2 Th 2:6,8), and since this prophecy has been clearly fulfilled in the history and development of the Roman Papacy, it is Scripture which reveals that the Papacy is the Antichrist.

THESES ON CHURCH FELLOWSHIP

Introduction to the Theses

Already during the early 1940s differences began to disturb the unity within the Synodical Conference on the doctrine and practice of church fellowship. Since 1872, when this confessionally sound federation of Lutheran synods was founded, the member synods were fully agreed on the fellowship principles that had brought them together. All held that complete confessional unity is the necessary scriptural basis for all practice of church fellowship, that is, for pulpit, altar, and prayer fellowship.

In the 1930s the Missouri Synod held meetings with the American Lutheran Church, a merger of Lutheran synods not in doctrinal agreement and not in fellowship with the Synodical Conference. Following the practice of the ALC, these meetings included joint prayer among all participants. Objections to this fellowship practice were answered by a Missouri Synod resolution in 1944, asserting that not all joint prayers are a practice of prayer fellowship. In regard to prayer, Missouri was allowing for a different practice and establishing different principles than those jointly held throughout its history by the synods of the Synodical Conference.

As this and other problems threatened the unity of the Synodical Conference, this body in its 1956 convention called upon its president to call a joint meeting of the union committees of the four member synods. One of the purposes was to draw up doctrinal statements faithful to Scripture in order to reestablish the fact that the synods of the conference were indeed in doctrinal agreement.

To the Wisconsin Synod's 1959 convention the Standing Committee on Matters of Church Union[1] could report that six meetings of the Joint Union Committees for a total of 18 days had been held since 1957. A doctrinal statement on Scripture and another on the Antichrist had been successfully completed. (See earlier sections in this booklet.) The subject of church fellowship had also been discussed on the basis of the presentation of theses by the Wisconsin Synod. These had been prepared by the subcommittee of eight in full consultation with the entire Standing Committee. In the meetings of the Joint Union Committees most of the points had met with approval. The Missouri representatives, however, were not ready to acknowledge "the scriptural correctness of the basic point of our Wisconsin Synod presentation . . . that all joint expressions and demonstrations of a common Christian faith—call them church fellowship or by any other term—are essentially one, that they involve a unit concept, and that they are therefore all [also prayer] governed by one set of principles"(*Proceedings*, 1959, p. 165). In view of the seriousness of this subject for the future relations of the two synods, the convention requested the Joint Union Committees to give primary consideration to the area of fellowship.

In 1960, the Missouri men submitted their "Theology of Fellowship" to the Joint Union Committees. On the crucial point noted above, this document spoke of a "growing edge of fellowship" and contended that "in reaching out to those not yet in confessional fellowship with us there is the possibility of the

---

[1]For the make-up of the Standing Committee and its eight-member subcommittee, see the Introduction to the Statement on Scripture.

beginning of the practice of fellowship." This was the start of what has become Missouri's position on "levels of fellowship." In the meetings in May 1960, after three days of discussions, the Wisconsin delegation recognized that the consideration of this subject had reached an impasse.

The doctrine of church fellowship became the primary divisive issue that resulted in the 1961 Wisconsin Synod resolution suspending fellowship with the Missouri Synod. The resolution recognized the "Theses on Church Fellowship" as "an expression of the scriptural principles on which the Wisconsin Evangelical Lutheran Synod has stood and which have guided it in its practice for many years." Since their appearance the theses have been and are still recognized as such.

For further reading:

"Essay on Church Fellowship," Carl Lawrenz, a detailed exposition of the scriptural basis of the "Theses on Church Fellowship," presented at the 1960 district convention of the Northern Wisconsin District and published in *Doctrinal Statements, 1970*.

"Fellowship Then and Now," a series of articles prepared by a subcommittee of the Standing Committee on Church Union for the *Northwestern Lutheran* and published in pamphlet form in 1960.

Both of these works and many others appear in *Essays on Church Fellowship*, Milwaukee: Northwestern Publishing House, 1996.

Church Fellowship: Working Together for the Truth, John F. Brug, Milwaukee: Northwestern Publishing House, 1996.

Theses on Church Fellowship

Preamble

Church fellowship is a term that has been used to designate both a *status* and an *activity*. Both usages lie very close together, and one flows out of the other. The two usages follow the general dogmatic distinction of *actu primo et actu secundo*.

Church fellowship can be *defined* as the *status* in which individuals or groups, on the basis of a common confession of faith, have mutually recognized one another as Christian brethren and now consider it God-pleasing to express, manifest, and demonstrate their common faith jointly.

Church fellowship can also be *defined* as the *activity* which includes every joint expression, manifestation, and demonstration of the common faith in which Christians (individuals or groups), on the basis of their confession, find themselves to be united with one another. (Mutual recognition of one another as Christian brethren is itself one such "joint expression" of common faith in which Christians on the basis of their confession find themselves to be united with one another.)

For very practical reasons, we have preferred to treat church fellowship in our theses as a term designating an *activity* since the inter-synodical tensions have to do more with church fellowship as an activity than as a status. Both as a status and as an activity, church fellowship needs to be distinguished from the spiritual fellowship of faith in the Holy Christian Church (*Una Sancta*) which it is meant to reflect but with which it cannot simply be identified. For in the case of hypocrites, who have not yet been revealed, church fellowship is still called for, though the fellowship in the Holy Christian Church (*Una Sancta* fellowship) is actually not existing. On the other hand, people may in God's sight be united in the fellowship in the Holy Christian Church (*Una Sancta* fellowship) and yet not have warrant to practice church fellowship here on earth.

We also felt that our definition of church fellowship was general enough to include both proper and improper practice of church fellowship, for the definition itself does not specify what constitutes an adequate confession on the basis of which individuals or groups may properly find themselves united in a common faith. For is there not in all church fellowship the assumption present that an adequate confession exists? Our presentation under the points of B sets forth what constitutes a proper confession, the marks of the Church *(notae purae)*, on the basis of which Christians may properly find themselves united in a common faith.

The Theses

Church fellowship is every joint expression, manifestation, and demonstration of the common faith in which Christians on the basis of their confession find themselves to be united with one another.

A. How Scripture leads us to this concept of church fellowship.
1. Through faith in Christ, the Holy Spirit unites us with our God and Savior. Gal 3:26; 4:6; 1 Jn 3:1.
2. This Spirit-wrought faith at the same time unites us in an intimate bond with all other believers. 1 Jn 1:3; Eph 4:4-6; Jn 17:20,21. Compare also the many striking metaphors emphasizing the unity of the Church, e.g., the body of Christ, the temple of God.
3. Faith as spiritual life invariably expresses itself in activity which is spiritual in nature, yet outwardly manifest, e.g., in the use of the means of grace, in prayer, in praise and worship, in appreciative use of the "gifts" of the Lord to the Church, in Christian testimony, in furthering the cause of the gospel, and in deeds of Christian love. Jn 8:47; Gal 4:6; Eph 4:11-14; Ac 4:20; 2 Co 4:13; 1 Pe 2:9; Gal 2:9; 5:6.
4. It is God the Holy Ghost who leads us to express and manifest in activity the faith which He works and sustains in our hearts through the gospel. Gal 4:6; Jn 15:26,27; 7:38,39; Ac 1:8; Eph 2:10.
5. Through the bond of faith in which He unites us with all Christians, the Holy Spirit also leads us to express

and manifest our faith jointly with fellow Christians according to opportunity: as smaller and larger groups, Ac 1:14,15; 2:41-47; Gal 2:9; as congregations with other congregations, Ac 15; 1 Th 4:9,10; 2 Co 8:1,2,18,19; 9:2. (Before God every activity of our faith is at the same time fellowship activity in the communion of saints. 1 Co 12; Eph 4:1-16; Ro 12:1-8; 2 Ti 2:19.)

6. We may classify these joint expressions of faith in various ways according to the particular realm of activity in which they occur, e.g., pulpit fellowship; altar fellowship; prayer fellowship; fellowship in worship; fellowship in church work, in missions, in Christian education, and in Christian charity. Yet insofar as they are joint expressions of faith, they are all essentially one and the same thing and are all properly covered by a common designation, namely, church fellowship.[2] Church fellowship should therefore be treated as a unit concept, covering every joint expression, manifestation, and demonstration of a common faith. Hence, Scripture can give the general

---

[2]Full attention needs to be given in this statement to the limiting terms: "insofar" and "joint." The "insofar" is to point out that it is indeed only in their function as joint expressions of faith that the use of the means of grace and such other things mentioned as Christian prayer, Christian education, and Christian charity all lie on the same plane. In other respects the means of grace and their use are indeed unique. Only through the means of grace, the gospel in Word and Sacrament, does the Holy Spirit awaken, nourish, and sustain faith. Again, only the right use of Word and Sacrament are the true marks of the church, the marks by which the Lord points us to those with whom He would have us express our faith jointly.

For anything to be a "joint" expression of faith presupposes that those involved are really expressing their faith *together*. This distinguishes a joint expression of faith from individual expressions of faith which happen to be made at the same time and at the same place. Certain things like the

admonition "avoid them" when church fellowship is to cease (Ro 16:17). Hence, Scripture sees an expression of church fellowship also in giving the right hand of fellowship (Gal 2:9) and in greeting one another with the fraternal kiss (Ro 16:16); on the other hand, it points out that a withholding of church fellowship may also be indicated by not extending a fraternal welcome to errorists and by not bidding them Godspeed (2 Jn 10,11; cf. 3 Jn 5-8).

B. What principles Scripture teaches for the exercise of such church fellowship.
1. In selecting specific individuals or groups for a joint expression of faith, we can do this only on the basis of their confession. It would be presumptuous on our part to attempt to recognize Christians on the basis of the personal faith in their hearts. 2 Ti 2:19; Ro 10:10; 1 Jn 4:1-3; 1 Sa 16:7.
2. A Christian confession of faith is in principle always a confession to the entire Word of God. The denial, adulteration, or suppression of any word of God does not stem from faith but from unbelief. Jn 8:31; Mt 5:19;

---

celebration of the Lord's Supper, the proclamation of the gospel, and also prayer, are by their very nature expressions of faith and are an abomination in God's sight when not intended to be that. When done *together*, they are therefore invariably joint expressions of faith. Other things like giving a greeting, a kiss, a handshake, and extending hospitality or physical help to others are in themselves not of necessity expressions of Christian faith. Hence, doing these things together with others does not necessarily make them joint expressions of faith, even though a Christian will for his own person also thereby be expressing his faith (cf. 1 Co 10:31). These things done together with others become joint expressions of faith only when those involved intend them to be that, understand them in this way, and want them to be understood thus, as in the case of the apostolic collection for the poor Christians at Jerusalem, the fraternal kiss of the apostolic church, and our handshake at ordination and confirmation.

1 Pe 4:11; Jer 23:28,31; Dt 4:2; Rev 22:18,19. We recognize and acknowledge as Christian brethren those who profess faith in Christ as their Savior and with this profession embrace and accept His entire Word. Compare Walther's "Theses on Open Questions,"[3] Thesis 7: "No man has the privilege, and to no man may the privilege be granted, to believe and to teach otherwise than God has revealed in His Word, no matter whether it pertains to primary or secondary fundamental articles of faith, to fundamental or nonfundamental doctrines, to matters of faith or of practice, to historical items or other matters subject to the light of reason, to important or seemingly unimportant matters."

3. Actually, however, the faith of Christians and its manifestations are marked by many imperfections, either in the grasp and understanding of scriptural truths, or in the matter of turning these truths to full account in their lives. We are all weak in one way or another. Php 3:12; Eph 4:14; 3:16-18; 1 Th 5:14; Heb 5:12; 1 Pe 2:2. Compare Walther's Thesis 5: "The Church militant must indeed aim at and strive for absolute unity of faith and doctrine, but it never will attain a higher degree of unity than a fundamental one." Cf. Thesis 10.

4. Weakness of faith is in itself not a reason for terminating church fellowship, but rather an inducement for practicing it vigorously to help one another in overcoming our individual weaknesses. In precept and example, Scripture abounds with exhortations to pay our full debt of love toward the weak.

---

[3] Dr. Walther's "Theses on Open Questions" are printed at the end of this doctrinal statement.

a. General exhortations. Gal 6:1-3; Eph 4:1-16; Mt 18:15-17.
b. Weakness in laying hold of God's promises in a firm trust. Mt 6:25-34.
c. Weakness with reference to adiaphora in enjoying fully the liberty wherewith Christ has made us free. Ro 14; 1 Co 8 and 9. The public confession of any church must [on the basis of Scripture] establish, however, which things are adiaphora, so that it may be evident who are the weak and who are the strong. Ro 14:17-23; 1 Co 6:12; 10:23,24.
d. Weakness in understanding God's truth, and involvement in error. Ac 1:6; Galatians (Judaizing error); Colossians (Jewish-Gnostic error); 1 Co 15; 1 Th 4:10-12,14; 2 Th 3:6,14,15; Ac 15:5,6,22,25. Note how in all these cases, Paul patiently built up the weak faith of these Christians with the gospel to give them strength to overcome the error that had affected them. Compare Walther's Theses 2, 3, 4, and 8.
5. Persistent adherence to false doctrine and practice calls for termination of church fellowship.
a. We cannot continue to recognize and treat anyone as a Christian brother who in spite of all brotherly admonition impenitently clings to a sin. His and our own spiritual welfare calls for termination of church fellowship (excommunication). Mt 18:17; 1 Co 5:1-6.
b. We can no longer recognize and treat as Christian brethren those who in spite of patient admonition persistently adhere to an error in doctrine or practice, demand recognition for their error, and make propaganda for it. Gal 1:8,9; 5:9; Mt 7:15-19; 16:6; 2 Ti 2:17-19; 2 Jn 9-11; Ro 16:17,18. If the

error does not overthrow the foundation of saving faith, the termination of fellowship is not to be construed as an excommunication. Moreover, an excommunication can only apply to an individual, not to a congregation or larger church group. The "avoid them" of Romans 16:17,18 excludes any contact that would be an acknowledgment and manifestation of church fellowship; it calls for a cessation of every further joint expression of faith. Cf. 1 Co 5:9-11. Compare Walther's Theses 9 and 10.

c. Those who practice church fellowship with persistent errorists are partakers of their evil deeds. 2 Jn 11.

From all of this, we see that in the matter of the outward expression of Christian fellowship, the exercise of church fellowship, particularly two Christian principles need to direct us: the great debt of love which the Lord would have us pay to the weak brother, and His clear injunction (also flowing out of love) to avoid those who adhere to false doctrine and practice and all who make themselves partakers of their evil deeds. Conscientious recognition of both principles will lead to an evangelical practice also in facing many difficult situations that confront us, situations which properly lie in the field of casuistry.

On the basis of the foregoing, we find it to be an untenable position

A. To distinguish between joint prayer which is acknowledged to be an expression of church fellowship and an occasional joint prayer which purports to be something short of church fellowship;

B. To designate certain nonfundamental doctrines as not being divisive of church fellowship in their very nature;

C. To envision fellowship relations (in a congregation, in a church body, in a church federation, in a church agency, in a cooperative church activity) like so many steps of a ladder, each requiring a gradually increasing or decreasing measure of unity in doctrine and practice.

"Theses on Open Questions" by Dr. Walther, 1868

(These theses are the ones on the basis of which the Wisconsin and Missouri Synods established fellowship.)

THESIS I. It cannot be denied that in the field of religion or theology there are questions which, because they are not answered in the Word of God, may be called open in the sense that agreement in answering them is not required for the unity of faith and doctrine which is demanded in the Word of God, nor does it belong to the conditions required for church fellowship, for the association of brethren or colleagues.

THESIS II. The error of an individual member of the Church even against a clear Word of God does not involve immediately his actual forfeiture of church fellowship, nor of the association of brethren and colleagues.

THESIS III. Even if an open error against the Word of God has infected a whole church body, this does not in itself make that church body a false church, a body with which an orthodox Christian or the orthodox church would abruptly have to sever relations.

THESIS IV. A Christian may be so weak in understanding that he cannot grasp, even in a case of a fundamental article of the second order, that an error which he holds is contrary to the Scriptures. Because of his ignorance he may also continue in his error, without thereby making it necessary for the orthodox church to exclude him.

THESIS V. The Church militant must indeed aim at and strive for complete unity of faith and doctrine, but it never will attain a higher degree of unity than a fundamental one.

THESIS VI. Even errors in the writings of recognized orthodox leaders of the Church, now deceased, concerning nonfundamental doctrines of the second order do not brand them as errorists nor deprive them of the honor of orthodoxy.

THESIS VII. No man has the privilege, and to no man may the privilege be granted, to believe and to teach otherwise than God has revealed in His Word, no matter whether it pertain to primary or secondary fundamental articles of faith, to fundamental or nonfundamental doctrines, to matters of faith or of practice, to historical matters or other matters subject to the light of reason, to important or seemingly unimportant matters.

THESIS VIII. The Church must take steps against any deviation from the doctrine of the Word of God, whether this be done by teachers or by so-called laymen, by individuals or by entire church bodies.

THESIS IX. Such members as willfully persist in deviating from the Word of God, no matter what question it may concern, must be excluded.

THESIS X. From the fact that the Church militant cannot attain a higher degree of unity than a fundamental one, it does not follow that any error against the Word of God may be granted equal rights in the Church with the truth, nor that it may be tolerated.

THESIS XI. The idea that Christian doctrines are formed gradually and that accordingly any doctrine which has not completed such a process of development must be counted among the open questions, militates against the doctrine that the Church at all times is strictly one, and that the Scripture is the one and only, but fully sufficient source of knowledge in the field of Christian religion and theology.

THESIS XII. The idea that such doctrines as have not yet been fixed symbolically must be counted among the open questions, militates against the historical origin of the Symbols, particularly against the fact that these were never intended to present a complete doctrinal system, while they indeed acknowledge the entire content of the Scriptures as the object of the faith held by the Church.

THESIS XIII. Also the idea that such doctrines in which even recognized orthodox teachers have erred must be admitted as open questions militates against the canonical authority and dignity of the Scriptures.

THESIS XIV. The assumption that there are Christian doctrines of faith contained in the Holy Scriptures, which nevertheless are not presented in them clearly, distinctly, and unmistakably, and that hence they must be counted with the open questions militates against the clarity, and thus against the very purpose or the divinity of the Holy Scriptures, which is offered to us as the divine revelation.

THESIS XV. The modern theory that among the clearly revealed doctrines of the Word of God there are open questions is the most dangerous unionistic principle of our day, which will lead consistently to skepticism and finally to naturalism.

THESES ON THE CHURCH AND MINISTRY

Introduction to the Theses

The Theses on the Church and Ministry in their present form were adopted by the Wisconsin Evangelical Lutheran Synod in 1969. They were the distillation of nearly a century of study, discussion, and debate.

In the late 1870s the Christian day school teachers of the Wisconsin and Missouri Synods in Wisconsin began to discuss the nature of their call. Where did their work in the church fit in the New Testament delineation of the public ministry? Was it a branch of the work of a pastor, who was to shepherd all the flock of which the Holy Spirit had made him an overseer (Ac 20:28)? Or was it an extension of parents' responsibility to bring up their children in the training and instruction of the Lord (Eph 6:4)?

Both pastors and teachers of the two sister synods in the Manitowoc, Wisconsin, area discussed the question in the mid-1880s. It was agreed that the teachers' work was divinely instituted since it involved the teaching of God's Word. But could it be identified with any of the offices in Ephesians 4:11 where pastors and teachers are mentioned? More study was needed.

At a pastors' conference in 1892, Wisconsin Synod Seminary Director Adolf Hoenecke, noting that the work of a Christian day school teacher is not specifically mentioned in the Scriptures, derived the teacher's call from the pastor's. In the discussion it was suggested that, since the teacher is called by the congregation, the teacher's work falls directly under the shepherding spoken of in Acts 20:28 and need not be considered an offshoot of the pastor's call to establish its divine nature.

In the following years the seminary faculty intensively studied the pertinent Scripture passages to answer the question: Is the office of pastor, apart from the apostolate, the only divinely instituted office in the church? Closely related was the question: Is the local congregation the only divinely instituted form of the church? Practical situations made the answer to these questions imperative.

Especially difficult was the so-called Cincinnati case. This involved some excommunications in a Missouri Synod congregation. When the district criticized the excommunications and upheld the district president's suspension of the pastors of the congregation, the congregation and its pastors applied for membership in the Wisconsin Synod. So Wisconsin was drawn into the case and had to consider: What happens when a synod's action conflicts with a congregation's excommunication? Which is supreme, a congregation or a synod?

The Missouri Synod's St. Louis seminary faculty entered the debate, objecting to articles published in Wisconsin's theological journal. These articles pointed out that God has prescribed no legal regulations for the New Testament church. Hence, as Acts 6:1-6 shows, the church is free to establish whatever forms of public ministry it in Christian wisdom and in keeping with good order and love considers useful. Likewise, in Christian liberty it can organize itself in whatever ways it chooses in accordance with these principles. The articles recognized that the pastorate of a congregation as we know it today cannot be equated with any office of the public ministry mentioned in the New Testament.

In the articles, it was noted that there is no passage in the New Testament which establishes the pastorate of a local congregation as the one divinely instituted form of the public ministry, nor is there a passage which establishes the local congregation as the one divinely instituted form of the church. Various kinds of public servants of the Word are Christ's gift to his church, as is clear from Ephesians 4:11, 1 Corinthians 12:28, and other passages, and the gathering of Christians into various groups is the work of the Holy Spirit, as Luther's Explanation of the Third Article states.

The St. Louis faculty, on the other hand, argued that the local congregation is the one divinely instituted form of the church and that a synod is a purely human organization. Likewise, it held that the office of pastor of a local congregation is the only divinely instituted form of the public ministry and all other forms are auxiliary to it.

Although, for convenience' sake, the one position was spoken of as the Missouri and the other as the Wisconsin position, in fact there were supporters of both positions in both synods. Representatives of the St. Louis faculty met with the Thiensville faculty in 1932 and drew up the "Thiensville Theses" as a preliminary step toward a settlement of the controversy. No further steps were taken, however. In 1946 the Synodical Conference established an Interim Committee to address these issues, but the question remained unsettled.

In the late 1950s new committees were appointed to attempt to settle doctrinal questions that were disturbing the unity in the Synodical Conference. The Wisconsin committee drew up the statement on church and ministry for these deliberations. The differences in the doctrine of church fellowship took center stage, however, and the issue of church and ministry never came before the group.

The theses do not address the question of whether women may serve in the public ministry. At the time of writing the issue of women pastors had not yet come to the fore. Because of the fact that for decades women had served in the public ministry as Christian day school and Sunday school teachers, it was taken for granted that they may serve in positions that do not involve exercising authority over men. The statement on "Scriptural Principles of Man and Woman Roles" adopted in 1993 specifically addresses this issue.

For further reading:
WELS Ministry Compendium, WELS Board for Parish Services, 1992.

"The Doctrine of Church and Ministry in the Life of the Church Today," Wilbert Gawrisch, essay at the 1991 WELS convention printed in *Proceedings of the Fifty-first Biennial Convention*, pp. 204-247.

Church–Mission–Ministry: The Family of God, Armin W. Schuetze, Milwaukee: Northwestern Publishing House, 1996.

"The Pastoral Ministry as a Distinct Form of the Public Ministry," Thomas P. Nass, *Wisconsin Lutheran Quarterly*, Vol. 91, No. 4 (Fall 1994), pp. 243-272.

Theses on the Church and Ministry

I. The Church

A. *The Church is the communion of saints*, the entire number of those whom the Holy Spirit has brought to faith in Christ as their Savior and whom through this gracious gift of a common faith He has most intimately joined together to form one "congregation" (Augsburg Confession VII, VIII), one body, one blessed fellowship.

As long as we keep the truth that the Church is the communion of saints in mind, everything that Scripture tells us about the Church will fall into its proper place and can be readily understood. At the same time all the false notions which men have entertained and still entertain concerning the Church are readily exposed.

Mt 16:16-18: Through his God-given faith in Jesus as his divine Redeemer Simon had become Peter, a building block laid on Christ the foundation rock to form a part of the growing edifice of Christ's Church.
Eph 2:19-22; Jn 10:16; 1 Co 1:2; 2 Co 1:1; 1 Th 1:1; Ac 2:47.

B. *The Church*, just because it is the communion of saints, the congregation of all true believers, *is of necessity invisible*, that is, it can be apprehended only by faith.

Ro 10:10; 1 Sa 16:7; 2 Ti 2:19. Since faith in Christ, which alone makes sinful human beings members of the Church, is a matter of the heart, God alone can discern all those who are really His.

We can judge others only on the basis of the profession of faith that they make in word and deed. Such a profession may be false and hypocritical. Hence the Church cannot be equated with any individual church organization whose members can be determined and tabulated by men on the basis of their outward profession. Just as little is it to be equated with the sum total of all such outward churches.

C. *The Church* of believers, though invisible, *is a blessed reality*.

It is not a mere platonic idea.

1. It is the object of God's gracious thoughts from all eternity. Jn 17:2,6,9,11,12; 13:18; Eph 1:4.
2. Everything that happens and that will happen is bound up with the gathering and completion of the Church. Eph 1:20-23.
3. It is a reality that is to be of great comfort and concern for us. Eph 2:18-22; 4:1-16; 1 Co 12.

D. *The Church*, the communion of saints, *is present* there *where the means of grace are in use*, where the Gospel is rightly taught and the Sacraments are rightly administered (Marks of the Church).
   1. It is *through the Gospel* (in Word or Sacrament) that the *Church has* received *its life*. All of its members have been born again by the incorruptible seed of the Word of God. Through the Gospel the spiritual life of all its members is sustained. *Through the Gospel the Holy Spirit* calls, gathers, enlightens, and sanctifies the whole Christian Church on earth, and keeps it with Jesus Christ in the one true faith. Jn 6:63; 3:5,6; 1 Pe 1:23-25; Ro 1:16; Tit 3:5; 1 Co 10:17; Jn 17:17,20.
   2. Not all, of course, who hear the Gospel believe. Mt 23:37; Ac 7:51; Heb 4:2; Augsburg Confession Art V. Yet the promise of the Lord stands that His word will not return to Him void, without accomplishing that which He pleases. Isa 55:10,11; Mt 28:18-20; 2 Co 2:14-16.
   3. Hence Scripture bids us to look for the Church there where the Gospel is in use, where people are gathered together both to receive its blessings and to bring them to others. Mt 18:20. Scripture designates such gatherings of people who profess faith in Christ and manifest it in the use of Word and Sacrament as churches. It does so, however, because of the believers found in their midst. Ac 4:32; 8:1; 5:1-11. Hypocrites are like chaff among the wheat, outwardly adhering to the company of believers but not a part of them. Until God exposes them, they, too, will be the *outward* recipients of the expressions of fellowship of the believers. 1 Co 5:13. Hence, when the New Testament speaks of the Church or of churches, the reference is

CHURCH AND MINISTRY

either to such as are known to God as believers (*ecclesia stricte dicta*, the communion of saints or a part of it present at any locality) or to such as are to be acknowledged as believers by us on the basis of their confession (*ecclesia late dicta*, the empirical church as we encounter it).

4. *The specific forms in which believers group themselves together* for the fellowship and work of the Church, the specific forms in which they arrange for the use of the means of grace in public worship, the specific forms in which they establish the public ministry, *have not been prescribed by the Lord to His New Testament Church.*

   a. It is the Holy Spirit who through the gift of their common faith leads the believers to establish the adequate and wholesome forms which fit every circumstance, situation, and need. 1 Co 3:21; 14:33,40. *God in His word merely bids them to gather together* (Heb 10:25) *and through their faith prompts them to do so.* Since believers ordinarily live at some local place, where they will desire to nourish their faith regularly through the means of grace, the local congregation will usually be the primary grouping of Christians.

   b. It is likewise the Holy Spirit who through the same bond of a common faith draws Christians together in Jesus' name in other groupings, and draws Christian congregations together in larger groupings, such as a synod, that they may share their mutual gifts and gain strength for certain phases of the great task of the Church, such as the training of pastors and teachers, the establishment and maintenance of mission fields. Ac 15; 1 Th 4:9,10; Ac 9:31 (the Greek text: the church in Judea, Galilee, and

Samaria); 1 Co 16:1 (the churches of Galatia); 2 Co 9:2 (Macedonia and Achaia); 2 Co 8:18,19 (Macedonian churches had a common worker and jointly elected a traveling companion for Paul); Ac 16:1,2 (Timothy's work praised by Derbe, Lystra, and Iconium).

c. *In essence the various groupings* in Jesus' name for the proclamation of His Gospel *all lie on the same plane.* They are all Church in one and the same sense, namely in this sense that on the basis of the marks of the Church the Lord lets us apprehend the presence of the *una sancta* (the Holy Christian Church) in each such grouping of people, and thus enables us to acknowledge them as gatherings of believers possessing the ministry of the keys with the right of exercising this ministry in accordance with the considerations of love and order. Here we need to distinguish between the possession of a right and the God-pleasing exercise of that right.

As the Holy Spirit leads Christians to group themselves together in Jesus' name (Jesus' name is His Gospel revelation), He *always* constrains them to do so in an orderly manner (1 Co 14:33,40) and in the spirit of love (1 Co 16:14). The Holy Spirit never leads Christians to group themselves together in Jesus' name for a competitive purpose so as to duplicate, hinder, or disturb that scope of the ministry of the keys which is already effectively provided for by a previously established grouping of Christians. Every added grouping of Christians in Jesus' name, as effected by the Holy Spirit, will be for the purpose of assisting the primary groupings in exercising certain phases of the ministry of the keys

CHURCH AND MINISTRY 47

more fully and more efficiently in keeping with the great commission of the Lord (e.g. in mission work, in Christian education, in the training of public servants of the Word, in Christian charity, in the supervision of doctrine and practice) or for the purpose of providing needed strengthening through Word and Sacrament which, because of special circumstances, is not adequately offered or cannot well be offered through already existing groupings (e.g. worship services at conferences and synodical conventions, ministry to students, to the handicapped, to the institutionalized, etc.).

The more fully also the secondary groupings of Christians remain conscious of their essential character as Church, the more keenly will they feel their *responsibility of functioning in accordance with love and good order* and thus carefully restrict themselves to those phases of the ministry of the keys which would otherwise fail to receive the attention that they deserve.

5. *The right use of Word and Sacrament* are the *true marks of the Church*, the marks by which the Lord points us to those with whom He would have us express the fellowship that we have in the communion of saints. Jn 8:31,32.

   a. The Lord in His Word admonishes us to withdraw our church fellowship from those who persistently teach, spread, condone error and demand recognition for it. Ro 16:17,18; 2 Ti 2:17-19; 2 Jn 9-11; Gal 1:8,9.
   b. Yet we rejoice in the fact that God in His grace and mercy can and does awaken, sustain, and preserve believers also in the midst of erring congregations and church bodies. 1 Ki 19:18. We remember,

however, that He does so not through the errors that are taught and condoned there, but only through the true Gospel message that is still heard in these erring churches. We are therefore incited to proclaim the pure Word of God with great zeal and faithfulness and also with meekness and love at every God-given opportunity, so that our testimony may perchance be heard also by those who are God's children in erring churches and help them in overcoming the errors with which they are surrounded.

Antithesis:

We hold it to be untenable to say that the local congregation is *specifically* instituted by God in contrast to other groupings of believers in Jesus' name; that the public ministry of the keys has been given exclusively to the local congregations.

II. The Ministry

A. *Christ instituted one office in His Church, the ministry of the Gospel.*

It is the task of proclaiming the Gospel in Word and Sacrament. Mt 28:18-20; Mk 16:15; Jn 20:21-23; Ac 1:8; 1 Pe 2:9; Lk 22:19,20. This office or service, the ministry of the keys, has been given to the Church, i.e., to the believers individually and collectively. Mt 16:19; 10:32; 18:18; 1 Pe 2:9.

Augsburg Confession V, 1,2: "That we may obtain this faith, the Ministry of teaching the Gospel and administering the Sacraments was instituted. For through the Word and Sacraments, as through instruments, the Holy Ghost is given, who works faith, where and when it pleases God, in them that hear the Gospel . . ."

Formula of Concord Solid Declaration XII, 30: "That the ministry of the Church, the Word preached and heard . . ."

CHURCH AND MINISTRY 49

B. *The purpose of this ministry is the edification of the Church*, by winning ever further sinners for Christ, and by building up those who are already members in Christian faith and life. Mt 28:18-20; Eph 4:11-14; 1 Co 12:7.

C. *From the beginning of the Church there were men especially appointed to discharge publicly* (in behalf of a group of Christians) the *duties of this one ministry*. Ac 13:1-3; 6:1-6.

D. *This public ministry is not generically different from that of the common priesthood of all Christians. It constitutes a special God-ordained way of practicing the one ministry of the Gospel.*
   1. All Christians are equal before God, neither superior nor inferior to one another, and all are equally entrusted with the same ministry of the Gospel. 1 Pe 2:9. Hence no one may assume the functions of the public ministry except through a legitimate call. Treatise on the Power and Primacy of the Pope 67-69: The authority to call *(ius vocandi)* is *implied in* the authority to administer the Gospel *(ius ministrandi evangelii)* given to the Church. Hence, it is proper to speak of the *derived* right of local congregations to call.
   2. God is a God of order; He wants us to conduct all of our affairs orderly (1 Co 14:33,40) and in the spirit of love (1 Co 16:14).
   3. Christians are not all equally qualified to perform publicly the functions of the ministry. The Lord sets forth the needed qualifications of those who are to perform publicly the functions of the ministry. 1 Ti 3:1-13; Tit 1:5-11. God gives to the Church men qualified for the various forms of the work required. Eph 4:7-16; Ro 12:6-8; 1 Co 12:4-11,28-31.

4. These gifts should be gratefully received and developed. 1 Co 12:31; 1 Th 5:19,20; 1 Ti 4:14; 2 Ti 1:6-9.
5. Thus these public ministers are appointed by God. Ac 20:28; Eph 4:11; 1 Co 12:28. It would be wrong to trace the origin of this public ministry to mere expediency (Hoefling).
6. There is, however, *no direct word of institution for any particular form of the public ministry.* The one public ministry of the Gospel may assume various forms, as circumstances demand. Ac 6:1-6. The specific forms in which Christians establish the public ministry have not been prescribed by the Lord to His New Testament Church. It is the Holy Spirit who through the gift of their common faith leads the believers to establish the adequate and wholesome forms which fit every circumstance, situation, and need. Various functions are mentioned in Scripture: 1 Ti 4:13; Eph 4:11; 1 Co 12:28; Ro 12:6-8; 2 Ti 2:2; Jn 21:15-17 (feeding); Ac 20:28 (watching); 1 Ti 3:2; 4:11; 6:2 (teaching); 1 Ti 3:5; 5:17 (ruling). In spite of the great diversity in the external forms of the ministerial work, the ministry is essentially one. The various offices for the public preaching of the Gospel, not only those enumerated above, e.g., in Eph 4:11 and 1 Co 12:28, but also those developed in our day, are all gifts of the exalted Christ to His Church which the Church receives gratefully and with due regard for love and order employs under the guidance and direction of the Holy Spirit for the upbuilding of the spiritual body of Christ; and all of them are comprehended under the general commission to preach the Gospel given to all believers.

Antithesis:

>We hold it to be untenable to say that the pastorate of the local congregation *(Pfarramt)* as a specific form of the public ministry is specifically instituted by the Lord in contrast to other forms of the public ministry.

RESOLUTION ON ABORTION

Introduction to the Resolution

On January 22, 1973, the U.S. Supreme Court declared abortion a constitutional right for all women. The WELS noted this sad development. In the February 25, 1973, issue of the *Northwestern Lutheran* an article read, "To approve of abortion as an expression of the right of a woman to have control over her body is not biblical. Neither man nor woman are masters of their own bodies. Both are responsible to God Himself for how they use them. . . . It is fervently hoped that no Christian woman will permit herself to be misled. Just because abortion may be legal, does not make it right."

The Lutheran Church—Missouri Synod, which had adopted its first pro-life resolution back in 1971, adopted another such statement in 1977. In 1978 the Evangelical Lutheran Synod adopted a resolution calling abortion a "grievous sin except in the rare instance of it being used to save a mother's life." That resolution resolved to "encourage its congregational members to confess publicly that the unborn child is a living person whose right to live must be protected."

Such public and formal proclamations may appear to be a startling departure from traditional conservative Lutheranism. In the past the Wisconsin Synod hesitated to take any such action in fear it may be a first step into a diluted theology marked by social activism. While that concern is legitimate, significant external factors compelled the WELS to be silent no longer.

First, the number of abortions had risen to a startling level. When abortion was legalized nationally in 1973, proponents suggested the abortion rate would not vary much from the expected 300,000 per year. Within a few years that number jumped to around 1.5 million annually and has remained at that level.

Secondly, the religious community appeared divided on the issue in the public forum. In 1974, one year after abortion was legalized, the U.S. Congress held public hearings on the prospect of a Human Life Amendment. Among those testifying were the following religious leaders: Bishop A. James Armstrong, president of the Board of Church and Society for the United Methodist Church; Mr. William Thompson, Executive Officer of the General Assembly of the United Presbyterian Church in the United States of America; and Rev. Sidney Lovett, Jr., Conference Minister for the Central Atlantic Conference of the United Church of Christ. Each spoke in favor of the right to abortion.

Thirdly, sprouting from the United Methodist Church came an organization called the Religious Coalition for Abortion Rights (RCAR). A 1978 pamphlet produced by the agency contained pro-abortion position statements of its member agencies. Among those agencies were the following: American Baptist Churches, Disciples of Christ, Lutheran Church in America, Presbyterian Church in the U.S., United Church of Christ and the United Methodist Church. Of particular concern is the prominent mention of Lutheran agencies in RCAR listings. Many publications listed the position statements of both the Lutheran Church of America and the American Lutheran Church as supporting a woman's right to choose abortion.

These factors raised questions in the public's mind concerning what God's Word says concerning abortion. Some clergy within the WELS also admitted that unclarity existed in the minds of some WELS members.

It was a lay member of First Evangelical Lutheran Church in Lake Geneva, Wisconsin, who assembled the original abortion statement in 1979 and submitted it for consideration through his pastor. In the committee and convention-floor discussion there were no voices speaking in favor of the right to abortion. The clarity of God's Word on abortion was not questioned. There was debate, however. The debate involved the question of whether the WELS should adopt resolutions on social issues.

Ultimately, the committee rewrote the resolution, making improvements. Perhaps most noteworthy was to go beyond the simple proclamation against abortion-on-demand and to request WELS members to support abortion alternative programs. The action became an important catalyst for the formation of WELS Lutherans for Life.

As time passes and religious entities that have strayed from God's Word cloud its truth in the public forum, the WELS may again be compelled to adopt other resolutions on social issues. In the meantime, it continues the twofold approach of (1) encouraging the WELS ministerium to continue the faithful proclamation of God's Word also when it addresses social issues and (2) encouraging the membership to be a positive influence in the battle against sin by their public testimony and vote.

Resolution on Abortion

WHEREAS 1) the Holy Scriptures clearly teach that the living yet unborn are persons in the sight of God and are under the protection of His commandment against murder (Job 10:9-11; Ex 20:13; Mt 5:21; Ge 9:6; Ps 139:13; Ps 51:5; Jer 1:5; Lk 1:41-44); and

WHEREAS 2) our hearts are grieved over the millions of unborn who are being murdered each year through the sin of willful abortion; and

ABORTION

WHEREAS 3) our synod has historically testified against abortion, except when it is medically necessary to save the life of the mother; therefore be it

Resolved, a) that we encourage the editors of our synodical periodicals as well as our pastors and teachers to continue fervently and faithfully to testify against abortion; and be it further

Resolved, b) that we continue to urge our membership to make God's will in this matter known to our fellowmen whenever the opportunity presents itself; and be it further

Resolved, c) that we encourage our membership to express their concern and compassion for distressed pregnant women by supporting the development of alternatives to abortion programs which are consistent with God's Word; and be it finally

Resolved, d) that we more zealously preach the Gospel of Christ which alone can change the wicked hearts of men and turn them from sin to righteousness.

STATEMENT ON THE LORD'S SUPPER

Introduction to the Statement

The 1970 edition of *Doctrinal Statements of the Wisconsin Evangelical Lutheran Synod* did not contain a statement on the Lord's Supper since there had been no controversy among us on this doctrine.

In September of 1977, however, a communication from President Wilhelm Petersen of the Evangelical Lutheran Synod expressed a desire of the ELS Doctrine Committee to meet with the WELS Commission on Inter-Church Relations in order to discuss a doctrinal question regarding Holy Communion which had arisen in the Lutheran Confessional Church in Sweden. This meeting was held on June 9–10, 1978, in West Allis, Wisconsin.

In the West Allis discussion on Holy Communion attention was given to questions dealing with the moment of the real presence, the function of the pastor's words of consecration, and the relationship between the pastor's recitation of the words of institution and Christ's original institution of the sacrament. Following this discussion the CICR felt that further elaboration and clarification was needed on some of the points under discussion. The CICR then drew up a lengthier statement on the subject titled "Lord's Supper: Consecration and Moment." Copies of this statement were forwarded to the ELS Doctrine Committee in January 1979, and a second joint meeting was held in Minneapolis on November 8–9, 1979.

In a third meeting between the two groups in Milwaukee on April 24, 1980, it was resolved to appoint a subcommittee from the ELS Doctrine Committee and the WELS CICR to draw up a statement of agreement on the subject under discussion.

Although each group formulated a separate statement, agreement was reached by the subcommittee on the basis of Thesis Nine of the ELS Doctrine Committee statement: "We hold that we cannot fix from Scripture the point within the sacramental *usus* when the real presence of Christ's body and blood begins, yet we know from Scripture and acknowledge in the Confessions that what is distributed and received is the body and blood of Christ." In this statement the sacramental union of Christ's body and blood and the bread and wine during the *usus* (consecration, distribution, reception), a matter which was not under discussion, is presupposed.

At its June 1981 convention in Mankato, Minnesota, the ELS adopted the following resolution:

"WHEREAS the theses on the Doctrine of the Lord's Supper composed by the Doctrine Committee of the Evangelical Lutheran Synod and the Statement on the Doctrine of the Lord's Supper composed by the Commission on Inter-Church Relations of the Wisconsin Evangelical Lutheran Synod are in agreement with each other, and with the Scriptures and the Lutheran Confessions, therefore, be it

Resolved, that we gratefully acknowledge the unity which continues to exist."

The CICR expressed its agreement with the foregoing resolution in a supplementary report to the 1981 WELS Convention held in Prairie du Chien, Wisconsin, in August. The convention endorsed the agreement with the adoption of a resolution of wider scope:

"WHEREAS	discussions with the Evangelical Lutheran Synod on the Lord's Supper and the Doctrine of the Church have been blessed by God; therefore, be it
Resolved,	a) that we thank God for these past discussions; and be it further
Resolved,	b) that we ask the Lord to continue to bless these contacts in the future."

Additional discussions on this matter between the ELS Doctrine Committee and the WELS CICR were held from time to time also in the years following 1981. These discussions have deepened the understanding and led to an ever-growing appreciation of this doctrine by our two synods.

The following is the Wisconsin Synod statement. It has been used by the CICR in discussions with other church bodies.

Statement on the Lord's Supper

In the matter under discussion we need to study Christ's words of institution in Matthew, Mark, Luke, and in 1 Corinthians, as well as St. Paul's additional statements about the Lord's Supper in 1 Corinthians 11 and 10. On that basis we can establish the following concerning the essence of the *usus* of the Lord's Supper (consecration, distribution, reception):

1. The real and substantial presence of Christ's body and blood during the *usus*.
2. The sacramental union of bread and wine and of Christ's body and blood during the *usus*.
3. The oral manducation of bread and wine and Christ's body and blood by *all* the communicants during the *usus*.

4. The real presence of the body and blood of Christ in the *usus* is brought about solely and alone by the power of Christ according to the words of institution, that is, by His command and promise.

We accept this statement (Point 4) with the understanding that:

    a) The real presence is effected solely by the original words of institution spoken by our Lord (*causa efficiens*) and repeated by the officiant at His command (*causa instrumentalis*).

    b) While we cannot fix from Scripture the point within the sacramental *usus* when the real presence of Christ's body and blood begins, we know from Scripture and acknowledge in the Confessions that what is distributed and received is the body and blood of Christ.

    c) The Confessions do not assert more as a point of doctrine than the above, which is clearly taught in Scripture.

SCRIPTURAL PRINCIPLES OF MAN AND WOMAN ROLES

Introduction to the Scriptural Principles

The 1960s and 1970s witnessed many changes in the attitude and practices of American society concerning male and female roles in life. These developments naturally led to questions being raised concerning the practices of the church in this matter. In response to such questions and to encourage a careful scriptural evaluation of the practices of our synodical schools, the Commission on Higher Education in April of 1978 adopted theses entitled "The Role of Man and Woman According to Holy Scripture." With the approval of the Conference of Presidents (COP) these theses and an exposition of them were submitted to the 1979 WELS convention. The convention, in turn, encouraged the districts of the synod to study them.

As a result of feedback from this study, the 1981 convention directed the COP to prepare a pamphlet addressing this subject. A committee of ten pastors, one from each district of the synod, was appointed to produce that pamphlet. The pamphlet which they produced, "Man and Woman in God's World," was published in 1985 with the approval of the COP. In 1987 "Man and Woman in God's World—An Expanded Study" was made available to provide more detailed exegetical background to the first pamphlet.

All three of these studies concluded that Scripture teaches that already at creation God established differences in male and female roles for this life on earth and that these differences in roles are still applicable today. A number of voices were raised in the synod, however, questioning whether such an "order of creation" was actually taught in Scripture.

The 1989 synod convention received a memorial requesting that "Man and Woman in God's World" be adopted as an official doctrinal statement of the synod and a counter-memorial suggesting that the pamphlet not be adopted as an official doctrinal statement since Scripture itself serves as an adequate statement of the doctrine. The convention resolved to receive "Man and Woman in God's World" as a correct exposition of the scriptural teachings in this matter. It urged the COP to prepare a brief, formal doctrinal statement for consideration at the 1991 convention.

In response the COP appointed a committee of five pastors to draw up such a statement. A preliminary draft of the statement was published in the *Northwestern Lutheran* with a request for comments and suggestions. A revised edition of the statement entitled "Scriptural Principles of Man and Woman Roles" was submitted to the convention by the COP. The convention accepted the statement as a correct exposition of scriptural doctrine and asked that members of the synod be given additional opportunity to suggest refinement of wording. It also asked the COP to authorize the preparation of study materials to help members of the synod study this issue in Scripture.

The committee responded by gathering additional suggestions for refinements in wording, and the COP submitted a revised edition of the statement to the 1993 convention, which adopted the reworded statement as a correct exposition of scriptural doctrine. The convention also requested a "brief, practical statement with a positive tone."

In response to the request of the 1991 synodical convention for study material, Prof. John Brug prepared a ten-lesson Bible study with teacher's manual entitled "A Bible Study on Man and Woman in God's World," which was published in 1992. In response to the request of the 1993 convention for a brief, practical statement, Pastor Walter Beckmann prepared "The Spirit in Which We Apply the Scriptural Roles of Man and Woman," which appeared in 1994.

"Scriptural Principles of Man and Woman Roles" is, thus, based on well over a decade of study by three different study groups. The doctrinal substance of its conclusions was adopted by three successive synodical conventions. This statement was not intended to be a comprehensive statement about scriptural roles for men and women. It is a brief doctrinal statement which addresses, both in a positive and negative way, specific issues which were points of controversy at the time the statement was composed. It strives to give balanced attention both to the spiritual equality which men and women share in Christ and to the different roles which God assigns to men and women in this earthly life. It emphasizes that the principles governing these different roles were established by God at creation and remain valid.

Scriptural Principles of Man and Woman Roles

In order to express our harmony in doctrine and practice with what God teaches in the Holy Scriptures about man and woman, we present the following statements as our confession:

Creation

1. God created man and woman in His own image. The divine image gave man and woman spiritual equality in their relationship to the Creator (Ge 1:26,27; Col 3:10; Gal 3:28).
2. In love God established distinct male and female responsibilities (Ge 2:7,18,22) for the man and

woman to whom He had given spiritual equality. These responsibilities involved headship for man and submission for woman. These roles demonstrated God's unchanging will for the complementary relationship of man and woman with each other. Two New Testament passages attest to this: 1 Co 11:3,8,9 and 1 Ti 2:12,13.

3. God established roles for man and woman in His creative plan before He united them in marriage and before they fell into sin (Ge 2:7,18,22; 1 Co 11:3,8,9). Therefore God's assigned roles apply beyond the marriage relationship and in every period of history.

The Fall

4. All commands of God and all roles established by God are for our good (1 Jn 5:3; Ps 19:8,11). To ignore or reject them harms our relationship with God and with each other (1 Pe 3:7; Eph 6:3; Ro 13:2-4).

5. When they sinned, man and woman lost the image of God and their perfect relationship with their Creator (Ge 5:1-3; Isa 59:2). Man and woman also lost their holy and harmonious relationship with each other (Ge 2:16,17; 3:12,16).

Restoration

6. God loved all men and women so much that He sent and sacrificed His Son to reestablish the holy relationship they once had with Him—Justification (Ro 5:8; 2 Co 5:18,19,21; Eph 4:24; Col 3:10).

7. Men and women enjoy equal status in their reestablished relationship with God when He brings them to faith in Jesus (Gal 3:26-29; Eph 6:9).

8. The restoration of God's image in us is a gradual

process which goes on throughout our earthly lives—Sanctification (2 Co 3:18; Eph 4:12-16). The Holy Spirit accomplishes this restoration by the power of the Gospel (Jn 17:17; 1 Th 3:13).

Headship

9. As God restores His image in us, we grow in our ability to live in our God-assigned roles for Jesus' sake (Eph 5:21–6:9; Col 3:18–4:1; 1 Pe 3:5-7).
10. Scripture teaches that headship includes authority (1 Co 11:3,10; Col 1:18; 2:10; Eph 1:22; 1 Ti 2:11,12). Authority should not be used to dominate but to serve others (Mt 20:25-28).
11. Christ exercised His headship with sacrificial love (Eph 5:25), humility (Php 2:5-8), and service (Eph 5:28,29), and asks all believers to carry out their roles of authority in the same way (Mt 20:25-28).
12. In applying the principle of role relationship, the church will emphasize the duties and responsibilities of men. God holds Christian men accountable for the use of the authority He has given them and will grant His blessings when men exercise this authority out of love for Christ (1 Pe 3:7; Col 3:19).
13. Believers in Christ live under His headship with willing submission, respect, obedience, and love toward those in authority (Eph 5:21–6:9).

In the Home

14. The role relationships of man and woman find their fullest expression in the close union of marriage. In a Christian home a husband and wife are partners and co-heirs of God's gracious gift of salvation (Eph 5:22-33; 1 Pe 3:1-7).

15. Since God appointed the husband to be the head of the wife (Eph 5:23), the husband will love and care for his God-given wife (1 Pe 3:7). A wife will gladly accept the leadership of her husband as her God-appointed head (Eph 5:22-24).
16. As the head of the wife and family the husband has the prime responsibility for the spiritual instruction of the family (Eph 6:4).

In the Church

17. The biblical principle of role relationship applies also to the gatherings of the church. All believers, men and women, will participate at gatherings of worship, prayer, Bible study, and service. The scriptural applications that a woman remain silent (1 Co 14:34) and that a woman should not teach a man (1 Ti 2:11,12) require that a woman refrain from participating in these gatherings in any way which involves authority over men.
18. In church assemblies the headship principle means that only men will cast votes when such votes exercise authority over men. Only men will do work that involves authority over men (1 Co 11:3-10; 14:33-35; 1 Ti 2:11,12).
19. All Christians, men and women, are to use their God-given gifts to serve each other (1 Pe 4:10). Women are encouraged to participate in offices and activities of the public ministry except where the work involves authority over men.

In the World

20. Christians also accept the biblical role relationship principle for their life and work in the world (1 Co 11:3; Eph 5:6-17). Christians seek to do God's will

consistently in every area of their lives. We will therefore strive to apply this role relationship principle to our life and work in the world.

21. Scripture leaves a great deal to our conscientious Christian judgment as we live the role relationship principle in the world. In Christian love we will refrain from unduly binding the consciences of the brothers and sisters in our fellowship. Rather, we will encourage each other as we seek to apply this principle to our lives in the world.

22. Because the unregenerate world is not motivated by the Gospel or guided by God's will (1 Co 2:14), we as Christians will not try to force God's will upon the world (1 Co 5:12). We will seek to influence and change the world by our Gospel witness in word and deed (Mk 16:15; Mt 5:16).

Since we affirm the preceding statements as biblical truths, we maintain that the propositions rejected below are contrary to the Word of God:

1. We reject the attempt to define male-female role principles only on the basis of biblical examples of human conduct because doctrine must be drawn from simple, direct statements of God's will.

2. We reject as a confusion of Law and Gospel the opinion that our spiritual equality before God restored by Christ (Gal 3:28) sets aside our distinctive responsibilities as guided by God's Law (1 Co 11:3).

3. We reject the opinion that relationships of headship and subordination are incompatible with a state of holiness (1 Co 11:3; 15:28). All New Testament passages regarding the role relationships are addressed to reconciled and sanctified men and women.

4. We reject the opinion that 1 Corinthians 11:7 teaches that only man, not woman, was created in God's image (cf. Ge 1:26,27).

5. We reject the opinion that distinct roles for man and woman were first ordered after the Fall in Genesis 3:16 (cf. Ge 2:7,18,22).

6. We reject the opinion that male headship and female submission apply only to marriage or only to marriage and the church (1 Co 11:3; 1 Ti 2:12).

7. We reject the opinion that the principle of role relationships taught in the New Testament was culturally conditioned and is not applicable today.

8. We reject the opinion that the principle of role relationships applies only to some people, only for some periods of history, or only to certain aspects of Christian life.

9. We reject the opinion that in the church assemblies only matters pertaining to the Word of God are authoritative.

10. We reject the opinion that the mutual submission encouraged by Scriptures for all believers (Eph 5:21; Mt 20:25-28) negates the exercise of male headship.

11. We reject the opinion that the word "head" as applied to Christ and man in the New Testament does not include authority.

12. We reject the opinion that every woman is always subject to every man. Other scriptural role relationship principles and the injunction, "We must obey God rather than men" (Ac 5:29), also govern our actions.

13. We reject arbitrary applications of the principle of the role relationships which do not take into account that customs which reflect these relationships as well as conditions of life may change (1 Co 11:6,16).

14. We reject the claim that the biblical statement "women should remain silent in the churches" (1 Co 14:34) forbids all speaking by women in the assemblies of the church.

With these statements of what we confess and what we reject we offer the prayer as Christian men and women that God will fill us with His Holy Spirit, giving to each of us a better understanding of and appreciation for our God-assigned responsibilities, that in loving service to Him and to each other we hallow His name and share in His mission in every God-pleasing way.